A Journey Through the Book of Jonah

Grumbling To Nineveh

Dr. Lee Ann B. Marino, Ph.D., D.Min., D.D.

Stumbling To Nineveh
A Journey Through The Book Of Jonah

Dr. Lee Ann B. Marino, Ph.D., D.Min., D.D.

Published by:
Righteous Pen Publications
(The righteousness of God shall guide my pen)
www.righteouspenpublications.com

All rights reserved. No part of this book may be reproduced or transmitted in any form or by any means, electronic or mechanical, or information storage and retrieval system without written permission from the author.

Unless otherwise noted, Scriptures taken from the Holy Bible, New International Version ®, NIV®, Copyright © 1973, 1978, 1984 by Biblica, Inc. ™ Used by permission of Zondervan. All rights reserved worldwide.

All passages marked KJV are taken from the Holy Bible, Authorized King James Version, Public Domain.

Scripture quotations marked GNT are from the Good News Translation in Today's English Version- Second Edition Copyright © 1992 by American Bible Society. Used by Permission.

Book Classification: Books > Religion & Spirituality > Christian Books & Bibles > Bible Study & Reference > Commentaries > Old Testament > Prophets

Cover and interior photo are in the Public Domain.

Copyright © 2015, 2022, 2025 by Lee Ann B. Marino.

ISBN: 194019721X
13-Digit: 978-1-940197-21-0

Printed in the United States of America.

God does not exist. For if I say that He exists, then I am already acknowledging doubt for His existence.
God is.
(Paul Tillich[1])

Spirit, lead me where my trust is without borders, let me walk upon the waters, wherever You would call me.
(*Oceans*, Hillsong United[2])

Table of Contents

	ACKNOWLEDGMENTS…………………………………	I
	FOREWORD………………………………………..	1
	INTRODUCTION (ABOUT THE BOOK OF JONAH)…………	7
1	RUNNIN' ON EMPTY (JONAH CHAPTER 1)……………...	11
2	WAITING FOR A SIGN…AND GETTING THE ONE YOU DON'T WANT (JONAH CHAPTER 2)………………………	29
3	STUMBLING TO NINEVEH (JONAH CHAPTER 3)…………	39
4	THE GOD YOU DON'T HAVE TO UNDERSTAND…BECAUSE HE IS (JONAH CHAPTER 4)…	47
	REFERENCES………………………………………………	55
	ABOUT THE AUTHOR………………………………………	59

Acknowledgements

I must thank all those who are part of Sanctuary International Fellowship Tabernacle – SIFT in Charlotte, North Carolina. As a growing community that's experienced plenty of ups and downs, I'm inspired by your commitment to God, to our work of inclusion and diversity, and to continuing in the faith, despite any challenges you face. Thank you for believing in and growing with us as we continue onward, as God reveals to us and builds us up, as we all overcome our own experiences with "stumbling to Nineveh!"

Foreword

Many of us have heard the story online about the little girl who challenged her science teacher about the story of Jonah and the whale: A little girl was talking to her teacher about whales in science class. The teacher said it was physically impossible for a whale to swallow a human, because even though it is a very large mammal, its throat is very small. The little girl stated that Jonah was swallowed by a whale, and she knew this to be a fact because they told her so in Sunday School. A very irritated teacher reiterated that a whale could not swallow a human; it was physically impossible. The little girl said, "When I get to heaven, I will ask Jonah." The teacher asked, "What if Jonah went to hell?" The little girl replied, "Then you ask him."

For those of you who went to Sunday School, you probably remember Jonah's story among the earliest Bible narratives you were taught in that atmosphere. The book of Jonah is often invoked as a cute Sunday School story to read to children. Many can recall the cute pictures of Jonah sitting in the belly of the whale, or riding the whale, or being thrown overboard from the ship. These pictures evoke powerful memories and concepts about Jonah and his experience as a prophet, but seldom do we ever hear the rest of the story, the heart of Jonah's experience, or why Jonah should cause each and every one of us to take a good, long look at our own spiritual inventory.

The story of Jonah is treated so much as a story for children's fodder that I think we forget Jonah was a prophet, a person who lived and had an assignment from God He was also someone with a genuine struggle. He wasn't just a guy who rode in the belly of the whale for a circus-like performance, to entertain and amuse people. The story of Jonah also does not end with Jonah sitting in the whale's belly for three days, nor does it begin in the belly of the whale. To many, Jonah is not any deeper than the pictures depicted in children's Bibles and Sunday School texts, a prophet who sat in the belly of a fish and…did nothing else, ever. From the teachings we had as children, you would think that Jonah's call was to prophesy to a whale's intestines.

I wonder if the reasons why we do not hear much about Jonah today are much deeper than Sunday School stereotyping, however. The book of Jonah doesn't get a lot of "yes" and "amens," especially nowadays. I almost feel like the book is treated with discomfort, because it addresses many things the church would rather pretend do not exist. Within the short, four-chapter book of Jonah, we find disobedience, racism, judgment, humanity, and challenges to God's authority, all of which are issues that today's church finds deeply uncomfortable. Jonah challenges the reader on faith, obedience, and calls each reader to examine the ways in which they are not quite measuring up in the eyes of God. Sharing the unique struggles of obedience, reluctant obedience, and the general feeling that one has when they just don't like nor agree with what God is asking of them to do, Jonah reveals the all-too-human equation in one's spiritual relationship with God.

Jonah dispels all notions that leaders are any better than anyone else. They are people who struggle with things despite their calls to ministry. They have points where God asks things of them that they simply cannot and will not find them within themselves to do. Jonah teaches us that these reasons do not matter. He reminds us of the constant call to die to oneself and look to something greater and more powerful so He can increase within us, and we can decrease (John 3:30). In a larger sense, he also reveals that Christians (including those with a ministry call) still have questions as they walk out their call of faith, day in and day out. Jonah shows a highly imperfect side to the believer: the one that questions God's judgments, that winds up in trouble due to disobedience, and that sits with existential questions about life that are neither simple nor easily answered. The book of Jonah challenges us to have a radical faith beyond mere observance, beyond our comfortable theologies, and beyond the attitudes and divisions that hinder us from reaching out to the world with the Gospel.

Not long ago, I attended a church service with a friend at a church we would brand as "seeker friendly." The church maintains a great atmosphere in terms of being a place to which people want to return and in making them feel welcome. It makes sure people desire to be there, no matter where they are at in their lives. It is obvious, however, from certain facets that people do not desire to change when they are there. I observed a man, smoking one last cigarette before going into the church. That same man was outside the church again, right after service dismissed, smoking another cigarette. The pastor of the church spoke of a long-time church member with a severe alcohol problem, presumed dead at one point, who was off on what was implied to be an alcohol "bender" and then re-appeared after the church went as far as to have a memorial service…with his same alcohol problem. It was obvious the people in that church were "comfortable" with God. They were comfortable with the issues they had, they were in no hurry or rush to resolve their own issues, and they were attending church where they were in the pursuit of those comforts. Nobody confronted their addictions, their problems, or their need for deliverance. They could attend, week after week, and remain in their same state, while never feeling the conviction to change. In discussing the service with someone else, my question became, "Where is the point when their encounter with God becomes uncomfortable?"

In every believer's life, and especially in every minister's walk, there should be that point where we become "uncomfortable" with God. The praise and worship music quiets down to the point of silence, we do not find what we need as easily from church on a regular basis, we have trouble handling our own disappointments and the feeling that we have been "failed" when our own theologies struggle to materialize in a convenient way, and we find it hard to accept the whole picture and purpose of Who God is beyond our comfortable theologies. We must come face-to-face with our human weaknesses, our shortcomings, our biases, and the areas in which we reluctantly obey or blatantly disobey God. We need to carefully step into a place of honesty with the ways in which we challenge God to "prove" Himself to us; in the ways of our walk that we are no better than the atheist or agnostic who almost dares God to do what they want, or they won't "believe" in Him or obey Him. We may dislike the deeper existential questions about the nature of God, if we really believe in God, or not, obedience to God, and following what God requires and requests of us to do, but that is not making them go away. No amount of atmospheric manipulation, seeker-friendly mindsets, or coffee before service is going to make the deeper questions of life – who are we, why are we here, how do we maintain a good relationship with God, what does God ask of us as believers, and how far will God expect of us in our obedience to Him – go away. Jonah is a book about one's relationship and relational perspectives of God, not in the sense of theology, but in the way God transforms our lives, our calls, our ministries if we have them, and the ways in which we create walls between one another to keep God Himself at a comfortable distance.

While Jonah may make people uncomfortable, the book of Jonah is not only timely, it is an essential read for anyone who struggles with the deeper existential questions as they walk with God. Jonah's experience reminds us of God's mercy, not just toward our enemies, but toward us, as well. It helps us to recognize our struggles and see that God either uses our testimony to testify of Him, or makes an example of us, when we clearly and obviously disobey. It also challenges us to look long and hard at ourselves and what we really know – and believe – about God, not just relying on exterior visuals, but the dialogue we have with Him and about Him when no one else is looking.

Jonah "stumbled" to Nineveh. He stumbled once he left Nineveh. He stumbled because he didn't understand the very nature of God and, as a human being, revolted against His Creator. In his stumbling, Jonah learned who he was, Who God was, and just how God needed to become sovereign in his life. God will never truly be God to us unless we go through this humbling process and "stumble" so He can become more to us than a cute musing and a nice theological ideal.

Introduction

ABOUT THE BOOK OF JONAH

Do you believe in God beyond your own concepts? Is your relationship with God strictly on your own terms? The book of Jonah forces us to examine these realities in our own walk with God. A deeply existential look at the struggle of human nature against the will of God, Jonah is an essential read for every serious believer who faces this inevitable spiritual struggle. From studying Jonah, we will learn the following:

- The inevitable human nature of every Christian and every Christian leader, and our call to overcome the different ways our human nature affects our ability to minister for God.

- The consequences of disobeying God.

- The subtle ways in which believers are frequently defying God and dwelling in places of unbelief.

- Why we cannot prove the existence of God and why that is relevant to our faith and obedience.

- The mercy and love of God is beyond human comprehension.

- The essential component of love, mercy, and non-bigotry in evangelism.

- Why God is beyond our level of understanding.

Position in the Bible

The Book of Jonah is in a group of twelve prophetic writings classified as the "Minor Prophets." Its classification as such does not mean Jonah is in any way of minor consideration or worth, but that the contents of the prophecies are far shorter than those of Isaiah, Jeremiah, and Ezekiel, whose writings are identified as the "Major Prophets." The book of Haggai follows the book of Obadiah and precedes the book of Micah.

Length

The Book of Jonah is four chapters long. Even in Bibles that sometimes number the verses differently, Jonah remains a four-chapter book, and the content is the same.

Author

The book of Jonah does not identify an author, but It is traditionally assumed to be written by the Prophet Jonah, himself. His name means "dove."

About the author

Even though the Prophet Jonah is mentioned in 2 Kings 14:25, what we know about the Prophet Jonah is found in the book of Jonah. All we learn from 2 Kings 14:25 is that Jonah was from the city of Gath-hepher. We do not learn much about his life, but we do learn about him as a person.

We see Jonah's very private struggles to overcome upbringing, bigotry, and to obey God. We even learn that obedience is not the end of one's experience with God. Giving us such keen insight into emotional states and spiritual battles, we learn the people God has called throughout history are not all that different from each and every one of us.

Time written

The book of Jonah seems to have been written between the eighth and fourth centuries B.C. It either reflects a prophetic time frame from around 8 BC or a situational timeframe from between the sixth to fourth centuries BC. Jonah himself would have lived during the reign of Jeroboam II (786-746 BC).

Who is Jonah for?

The narration of Jonah is for all believers. It gives us specific insight into the challenges human beings face as they follow God in their lives. It gives us special insight into the narrative mind when it comes to leadership obedience. The book of Jonah shows us the mind of the prophet and the things the evangelist must overcome in order to reach the world with the Gospel. The book of Jonah reveals crisis of faith, personal doubt and unbelief, and how bigotry and disobedience keep the church from reaching out to others.

History

The book of Jonah covers an unknown specification of time in the post-exilic period, under the reign of Jeroboam II. Jonah preached in the city of Nineveh, which was the capital of the Assyrian Empire. Assyria had a history of opposition with Israel, taking Israel captive in 722-721 BC. Nineveh was a large city by ancient standards and was most likely financially prosperous. This city was captured by the Babylonians and Medes in 612 BC.

Context

The book of Jonah focuses mainly on Jonah's personal battle with God. It is a story of faith, of unbelief, of signs and wonders, and the signs and wonders God works all the time, but people do not consider "praiseworthy." He did not want to obey God's call to minister unto the people of Nineveh. He went as far as to defy God's command to him, and then found himself the example of disobedience. Even though Jonah did go on to obey God, he still resented the outcome of his reluctant obedience. Jonah's dialogue with God, his internal struggles, his feelings, emotions, and the resentment he had, even when he did what he was supposed to do, call us to look at ourselves and examine just how we feel about the Almighty when His ways are clearly beyond our own.

Chapter One

RUNNIN' ON EMPTY
(JONAH CHAPTER 1)

Key verses

- **Verse 2**: *"Go to the great city of Nineveh and preach against it, because its wickedness has come up before Me."*

- **Verse 3**: *But Jonah ran away from the LORD and headed for Tarshish. He went down to Joppa, where he found a ship bound for that port. After paying the fare, he went aboard and sailed for Tarshish to flee from the LORD.*

- **Verses 10-12**: *This terrified them and they asked, "What have you done?" (They knew he was running away from the LORD, because he had already told them so.) The sea was getting rougher and rougher. So they asked him, "What should we do to you to make the sea calm down for us?" "Pick me up and throw me into the sea,"* *he replied, "and it will become calm. I know that it is my fault that this great storm has come upon you."*

- **Verse 15:** *Then they took Jonah and threw him overboard, and the raging sea grew calm.*

- **Verse 17:** *But the LORD provided a great fish to swallow Jonah, and Jonah was inside the fish three days and three nights.*

Words and phrases to know

- **Word of the Lord:** From two Hebrew words: *dabar*, which means, "speech, word, thinking, thing;"[1] and *Yehovah,* which means, "the existing One; the proper Name of the one true God."[2]

- **Jonah:** From the Hebrew word *Yonah,* which means, "'dove;' son of Amittai and a native of Gath-hepher; 5th of the minor prophets who prophesied during the reign of Jeroboam II and whom God sent also to prophecy to Nineveh."[3]

- **Nineveh:** From the Hebrew word *Niyneveh* which means, "abode of Ninus; capital of the ancient kingdom of Assyria; located on the east bank of the Tigris river, 550 miles (880 km) from its mouth and 250 miles (400 km) north of Babylon."[4]

- **Preach against:** From two Hebrew words: *qara*, which means, "to call, call out, recite, read, cry out, proclaim;"[5] and *'alah,* which means, "to go up, ascend, climb."[6]

- **Wickedness:** From the Hebrew word *ra'*, which means, "bad, evil; evil, distress, misery, injury, calamity; evil, misery, distress, injury."[7]

- **Ran away:** From the Hebrew word *quwm*, which means, "to rise, arise, stand, rise up, stand up."[8]

- **Tarshish:** From the Hebrew word *Tarshiysh,* which means, "yellow jasper;" son of Javan; a Benjamite, son of Bilhan; one of the wise men close to king Ahasuerus of Persia; a city of the Phoenicians in a distant part of the Mediterranean Sea to which the prophet Jonah was trying to flee; site unknown but perhaps in Cyprus or Spain; a city somewhere near and accessible to the Red Sea to which ships constructed at Ezion-geber on the Elanitic Gulf on the Red Sea were to sail."[9]

- **Joppa:** From the Hebrew word *Yaphow,* which means, "beautiful;" a town on the southwest coast of Palestine in the territory of Dan; became primary port of Jerusalem during reign of Solomon."[10]

- **Violent storm:** From two Hebrew words: *gadowl,* which means, "great;"[11] and *ca`ar,* which means, "tempest, storm, whirlwind."[12]

- **Afraid:** From the Hebrew word *yare'* which means, "to fear, revere, be afraid; to shoot, pour."[13]

- **Sleep:** From the Hebrew word *radam*, which means, "to be asleep, be unconscious, be in heavy sleep, fall into heavy sleep, be fast asleep."[14]

- **Cast lots:** From two Hebrew words: *naphal,* which means, "to fall, lie, be cast down;"[15] and *gowral,* which means "lot; portion."[16]

- **Hebrew:** From the Hebrew word *'Ibriy,* which means, "one from beyond; a designation of the patriarchs and the Israelites; a designation of the patriarchs and the Israelites."[17]

- **My fault:** From the Hebrew word *shel* which means, "who, which."[18]

- **Sacrifice:** From the Hebrew word *zebach*, which means "sacrifice."[19]

- **Fish:** From the Hebrew word *dag*, which means, "fish."[20]

- **Swallow:** From the Hebrew word *bala'*, which means, "to swallow down, swallow up, engulf, eat up."[21]

- **Three days:** From two Hebrew words: *shalowsh*, which means, "three, triad;"[22] and *yowm*, which means "day, time, year."[23]

- **Three nights:** From two Hebrew words: *shalowsh*, which means, "three, triad;"[24] and *layil*, which means, "night."[25]

Jonah 1:1-3

The Word of the LORD came to Jonah son of Amittai: Go to the great city of Nineveh and preach against it, because its wickedness has come up before Me." But Jonah ran away from the LORD and headed for Tarshish. He went down to Joppa, where he found a ship bound for that port. After paying the fare, he went aboard and sailed for Tarshish to flee from the LORD.

(Related Bible references: Genesis 10:11, Joshua 19:46, 2 Kings 14:25, 2 Chronicles 9:21, Isaiah 23:1, Jeremiah 10:9, Ezekiel 4:4-8, Hosea 1:2-3, Joel 2:32, Nahum 1:1, Zephaniah 2:13, Matthew 12:40-41, Matthew 16:4, Luke 11:30, Acts 2:21, Acts 9:36, Acts 10:5, Acts 14:15, Romans 10:12-13, 1 Corinthians 1:2, Ephesians 2:14-22, Hebrews 10:38, James 5:4, Revelation 18:5)

The book of Jonah opens without much fanfare. It, in its very direct style, gets right to the point. It doesn't matter how Jonah spent his childhood, or what he liked to do in his spare time. We know from 2 Kings 14:25 that Jonah was a prophet, and a prophet of enough reputation that people recognized and considered his ministry to be "relevant." He had a history of stating things within the realm of the prophetic, and that means people would have known his prophetic ministry. Alas, that's about all we know about Jonah's background: he was a prophet. He spent his life in obedience to God, speaking the Word of God to the people.

...or did he?

I'm not going to presume to know what Jonah's ministry was like prior to what we find in the book of Jonah...but the response Jonah gave to God – at more than one point in this short, four-chapter book – reveals someone who had issues with his calling and issues with God in a larger and deeper way. He knew about God and that God was there, but didn't approve of God's actions when His grace or favor was extended to the "wrong kind" of people. Jonah was somebody who was clearly called by God. He knew the voice of God in his life, he knew when God was telling him to do something, and he knew what God was instructing, saying, or commanding. Jonah didn't have the excuse that he didn't recognize God's voice in his life, as he had spent years in prophetic training. It's obvious Jonah wasn't a "newbie" at this. It's just really evident he didn't want to do what God told him to do. Jonah and God went way back, and Jonah and God obviously disagreed at times. How Jonah handled his disagreements prior to this point is unknown...but I can imagine, as one who has dealt with leaders for many years...that it, most likely, was not always pretty.

The book of Jonah is the only detailed account we have of Jonah's situation, and it begins just like it states above: God told Jonah to do something, and Jonah blatantly disobeyed God. He knew he'd heard from God, he knew it was God...and he just didn't think he had to do it.

The majority of teaching we hear around Jonah paints the prophet in a particularly disrespectful light. Jonah is frequently spoken of as having "ran" from his call. This is clearly not the case, given Jonah had been a prophet with a track record before he was called to Nineveh. He didn't run from being a prophet overall; he just ran from a specified assignment. He wasn't afraid and wasn't a coward; he didn't want to do what God asked of him. Before we seek to judge Jonah, we need to realize that Jonah represents every single believer who has run from God in disobedience at one point in their lives, or another. Even his name, which means "dove,"[26] indicates a certain passivity, someone who didn't want to confront things in his life and didn't want to confront things in his ministry. Every single one of us has "backed down" from a God-ordained or ordered requirement at some point in time. Instead of judging Jonah, we need to judge and examine ourselves.

Jonah was called by God, yes, but he was a human being called by God. Let's underline that key term: he was a <u>human being</u>. Being called by God did not turn him into a god, nor did it make him divine. He was still a person, with thoughts, feelings, insights, and opinions about what God asked of him. He had his own free will and was free to follow it as he desired. Being called did not give Jonah a uniquely divine perspective, especially if we properly understand the role of the prophet in the Old Testament. Old Testament prophets were given words and illustrations directly from God and were asked to do many things that were seen as culturally or morally reprehensible. What makes the book of Jonah unique is that we can see his response to God's orders. While we never hear about Hosea's balk when God told him to marry a prostitute (Hosea 1:2-3) or Ezekiel's protests to baking food with fecal matter for over a year (Ezekiel 4:4-8), we clearly see Jonah's human response to what God asked of him.

Before we are quick to judge Jonah's actions, let's be honest with ourselves: there is a little bit of Jonah in every one of us. Every single one of us has run from an assignment, a purpose, or a calling from God because there was something within it that was distasteful to us. Whether it was as simple as refusing to reach out to a friend or relative or something larger, such as running from a ministry call, we've all been there. We've really been there when the assignment is to someone we don't like, or feel should be saved. Like Jonah, we might have been gifted or maybe even anointed, but we didn't want to confront the things within us that were revealed in God's purposes for us. The call of God challenges us; it causes us to stumble our way there, learning to rely on God even more. To obey God, we must address our own biases, dislikes, and avoidances. To get to this point, we must first feel human.

...But we don't want to feel "human." We spend much of our spiritual lives trying to avoid our humanity. It's our deepest hope that spiritual sounds and appearances will drown out the aspects of ourselves that are further away from God than we might like to admit. We don't want to be in Jonah's position, forced to realize there are things about us that our gifts and abilities don't cover up. We have issues to root out, things we can't conveniently gloss over with Jesus and call it done. God forces our humanity through our call as we recognize what we have to do and struggle through the pains of the flesh to fulfil it.

In the midst of this humanity, however, we learn something important from Jonah's experience: His disobedience did not cause God to revoke His call on Jonah's life. Jonah, as he disobeyed, protested, clawed, kicked, and screamed was still called to be a prophet. The assignment did not change, his gifts did not diminish, and the call on his life did not go away. He could run as fast as he wanted to from God in the opposite direction, but God's call would find him out.

"Run" is exactly what Jonah did. The Bible is so explicitly detailed in each of Jonah's actions. Jonah wasn't having a slip-up or a bad day; he was deliberate in his disobedience of God. God told him to go to Nineveh. He got himself a ticket, got on a ship going in the opposite direction, and had absolutely no guilt nor fear for his deliberate actions. This is most ironic, because Jonah didn't want to go to Nineveh out of judgment, bigotry, and bias. He looked down on the people of Nineveh as less than he was, because they weren't Hebrews, and he was. He saw them as "sinners," unworthy of God's presence and forgiveness…while the whole time, he was himself sinning! He acted in just as much wickedness and disobedience as they did, Hebrew or not.

Jonah had baggage; his baggage was evident in how he behaved. How many of us do the same thing? How many of us are here, there, and everywhere, ignoring the commands of God or blatantly disregarding them because of our prior bigotries or biases? So many defend their bigotries by saying they were raised that way or it's just the ways of their culture…but it's obvious that excuse doesn't work with God. The evidence of that is in Jonah's ministry. You can't be called to the nations and be a bigot. To properly understand why Jonah was behaving like a bigot, we need to understand how that bigotry evolved in the first place.

If we look at the Old Testament and the Gospels of Matthew, Mark, Luke, and John as found in the New Testament, we can learn one key thing: the Israelites, those of the Jewish religion, thought a lot of themselves in that time. They believed the problems they had were not a result of their own doing, but due entirely to the persecutions around them. Ignoring command after command to repent and turn once again to the commands of God, Israel was, time and time again, turned over to its enemies. Time after time, Israel succumbed to the foreign gods, marrying foreign women, and bowing to foreign interests, priorities, and idols...and every single time, they blamed others for their own actions. The nation of Assyria, whose capital was Nineveh, was one of these nations. Known for their cruelty and strength in battle, Assyria was one of those nations that Israel feared, yet still picked up many of their pagan practices. Ignoring God's command to repent, Israel was turned over to Assyria.

It's not hard to fathom that, because Israel didn't want to be accountable for its own actions, that it saw Assyrians as their "problem." Even in days gone by, people stereotyped. Everyone else was their problem, everyone else was the reason they did what they did, and everyone else was the reason that they suffered. Seeing Assyria as an enemy, the people of Nineveh would have been seen as enemies, as well, and the people would have been hated. I'm not discounting the fact that the Assyrians were cruel and vicious, and I am also not discounting that they were a hardened people. But I am discounting this as giving anyone some sort of right to be biased against every single person in an entire nation because you don't want to obey God.

What does a stereotype sound like? "All Italians are in the mob." "All black people are violent." "All people on welfare are lazy and don't want to work." "All gay people want to abolish straight marriage." "All German people are Nazis." "All Muslims hate Americans." It's not as all deep as people try to make it out to seem. Many people use stereotypes on a regular basis and aren't even aware they are doing it, because it is so ingrained in the culture. Common, yes. Acceptable for Christians, no.

Stereotypes, judgments, bigotries, and biases of all sorts start with one's inability to take responsibility for themselves. It's easier to blame "them" rather than "us" and to believe someone else is the cause of all the world's evils. Wrongdoing, evil, and sinful behavior start when each and every one of us engage in such, not with what someone else is doing wherever they are. As we can see from the book of Jonah, bigotries and biases are not just a "worldly" thing found among "other" people. Jonah's biases need to call us to modern times and the issues of race, sexism, and bigotry of all sorts in church. We are fooling ourselves if we think these things do not exist in our modern systems, yet I meet all too many people who don't want to talk about, hear about, or address these issues within church. Any time there is mention of an issue as pertains to the injustices of women, people who are of a different race, or someone else, someone is always there, trying to straighten you out, and make it sound more like a "human" issue than one specified to the group you are speaking about. Churches today are still largely segregated, and people today desire to pretend that racism, sexism, and other issues simply do not exist, at least not within church. Nothing could be further from the truth. Examples of such include:

- Both the Methodist and Southern Baptist churches divided over slavery during the Civil War. Many other denominations divided and continue to divide over issues pertaining to the ordination of women, inclusion of queer individuals, and political issues..

- The early Pentecostal Movement was branded as heresy and "indecent" because it was racially integrated.

- During the Ferguson, Missouri riots after the shooting of Michael Brown, an unarmed, African American teenager preparing to go to college, by a Caucasian police officer who was never penalized for his crime, numerous so-called "Christian" men and women gathered to "pray for" and "encourage" the cop who shot this young man. They also raised money for him to exceed that given to the family of Michael Brown. In doing so, they said that such a display of police brutality was perfectly acceptable.

- After the not guilty verdict in the Trayvon Martin-George Zimmerman case and the release of officer Darren

Wilson (police officer who shot Michael Brown, an unarmed teenager in Ferguson, Missouri) and officer Daniel Pantaleo (the officer who put Eric Garner in an illegal choke hold unto his death), the divide between white and black Christians became more and more poignant as Caucasian believers told African-American believers to "get over it" and "justice was done." Even more argued that Trayvon Martin, Michael Brown, and Eric Garner were up to "no good," even when no such evidence existed to support the theories that these men were seeking to harm or violate the officers in question or other individuals around them.

- More than once, in our modern times, I have seen people grow irate in blaming women for incidents of domestic violence. Women are blamed for "getting up" in a man's face, or for speaking her feelings or her mind, or "making" him grow to a point where he does not control his anger. Instead of giving him responsibility for his behavior, women are constantly told, in no uncertain terms, it is "their fault."

- Repeatedly I hear various movements blamed for other things. Women who work are blamed for the "breakdown of the family," foreigners are blamed for disease outbreaks, feminists are blamed for gay marriage and for men not behaving responsibly, fast-food outlets are blamed for obesity, teachers are blamed for students' poor test scores…

…and so on, and so forth. Never-ending, never changing, and never resolving itself…without God's intervention.

I recently met a woman who complained of there not being a Pentecostal Holiness church in the city of Raleigh. I found this strange, because while I could only recall one church specifically referencing itself as "Pentecostal Holiness" (and it was quite a way outside of Raleigh), I could think offhand of at least five Pentecostal churches that emphasized holiness in southeast Raleigh. It didn't take long for me to realize that it's not that the churches aren't there, it's that she was unwilling to go to "that side of town" for church because it was a predominately African American sector of the city. Her attitude reflected a greater problem that doesn't seem to go away because too many of us are not dealing with the reality that it is there, alive, well, and thriving under doctrines of prosperity and middle-class aspirations. Many people in church today claim to be "called to the nations," but can't make their way across the street, to the south portion of their street (or vice versa), or even across town, because something down there causes their lifestyle upset or discomfort. Jonah teaches us exactly what it means to be "called to the nations:" You can't go the nations and be a bigot, because God doesn't tolerate bigotry. It doesn't matter how gifted you may be, how well you are able to flow in a spiritual gift, or how "anointed" you are. If you have issues with bias or bigotry of any sort, you are going to have to deal with them if you ever desire your ministry to be effective. Let's remember what happened to Jonah, shall we, when he wasn't willing to deal with his biases and get over them. In church today, God hasn't changed His mind about it. If anything, God has more to say about it than He did back then. Ephesians 2:14-22 states:

"For He is our peace, Who hath made both one, and hath broken down the middle wall of partition between us; Having abolished in His flesh the enmity, even the law of commandments contained in ordinances; for to make in himself of twain one new man, so making peace; And that He might reconcile both unto God in one body by the cross, having slain the enmity thereby: And came and preached peace to you which were afar off, and to them that were nigh. For through Him we both have access by one Spirit unto the Father. Now therefore ye are no more strangers and foreigners, but fellowcitizens with the saints, and of the household of God; And are built upon the foundation of the apostles and prophets, Jesus Christ Himself being the chief corner stone; In whom all the building fitly framed together groweth unto an holy temple in the Lord: In Whom ye also are builded together for an habitation of God through the Spirit." (KJV)

We understand this passage to literally be about Jew and Gentile, which yes, it is about. But beyond that, the Gospel is called "the Gospel of reconciliation" for a reason. If all people and nations are to call upon the Lord (Joel 2:32, Acts 2:21, Romans 10:12-13, 1 Corinthians 1:2), that means the enmity that exists between all people is clearly what was spoken of here. Jews and Gentiles weren't the only groups who faced hostility, one to another. The wars of this world, conquering, fighting, and striving for control throughout the ages prove the entire world needed a good old-fashioned reconciling. Within Jesus' very Body, crucified on the cross, every stereotype, every racist or sexist thought, every action or enmity done in the name of superiority, died there with Him.

This isn't just good propaganda for a council on ecumenism. God's desire is that His people are in unity with one another, regardless of the political and national divisions we claim in this world. It is not impossible for many people to come together and embrace His Son and one another if we abide by His principles: love, an end to hostility, and the promise of the Gospel to change lives. Every one of us has the transformation of Christ in common if we have truly been crucified with His Son. If we do not get over our own social biases, God will put us in a place where we must confront ourselves and the reasons why stereotypes and bigotries are more important than the work of Jesus in our lives.

Jonah clearly didn't have it all figured out. He didn't understand, or know, God as he needed to for his ministry to be as effective as it could be. He might have been accurate in terms of his prophecies, but that is different from it being effective. Someone who is a prophet or has a prophetic gift may get the details right, they may call things just as they are – but that does not mean their ministry bears the fruit it should. Jonah clearly had a gift, a gift from God, that was accurate. He was also a bigot, judgmental, and disobedient to God. He didn't have a reverential fear of God, an awe of Him, a boundary or realization that God's gift within Him is what made him the prophet he was. All he knew was God asked something of him…and he was not going to do it. Period.

Jonah 1:4-10

Then the LORD sent a great wind on the sea, and such a violent storm arose that the ship threatened to break up. All the sailors were afraid and each cried out to his own god. And they threw the cargo into the sea to lighten the ship. But Jonah had gone below deck, where he lay down and fell into a deep sleep. The captain went to him and said, "How can you sleep?" Get up and call on your god! Maybe he will take notice of us, and we will not perish." Then the sailors said to each other, "Come, let us cast lots to find out who is responsible for this calamity." They cast lots and the lot fell on Jonah. So they asked him, "Tell us, who is responsible for making all this trouble for us? What do you do? Where do you come from? What is your country? From what people are you?" He answered, "I am a Hebrew and I worship the LORD, the God of heaven, Who made the sea and the land." This terrified them and they asked, "What have you done?" (They knew he was running away from the LORD, because he had already told them so.)

(Related Bible References: 1 Samuel 14:42, Nehemiah 9:6, Psalm 19:8, Psalm 78:26, Psalm 95:5, Psalm 96:4-5, Psalm 103:19, Psalm 107:6, Psalm 107:25, Psalm 112:1, Psalm 115:16, Psalm 136:26, Psalm 146:6, Proverbs 16:33, Proverbs 18:18, Ecclesiastes 12:13, Isaiah 41:29, Amos 4:13, Zephaniah 2:3, Revelation 15:4)

The greatest realization we need to have – if we gain no other insight from the words of this section of Scripture – is the way in which Jonah's theology suited his beliefs. After setting out on his own course of action, Jonah saw fit to go to sleep. He didn't sit up all night, worrying that there would be consequences for his actions. He didn't pray or converse with God about his concerns pertaining to his disobedience. It never occurred to Jonah that his actions might have consequences for other people, like those on the boat he used to flee in the opposite direction of obedience. Jonah, at this point, didn't even have a repentant heart. He simply carried himself to bed and slept well enough to comfort himself in a deep sleep, so much so, he was totally ignorant to the winds, waves, and chaos that was ensuing around him.

As Christians, we must be very careful to make sure that our theologies haven't placed us in a comfortable position where God reflects our image, instead of us reflecting His. There are many ways in which we fashion God for ourselves, making us out to be more relevant, important, or essential than we oftentimes are. Yes, we are important to God, but we are not more important to God's plan than God Himself. If we don't choose to obey God's leading, God can either raise up an obedient servant in our place, or more likely, force us to deal with ourselves.

This is exactly where Jonah found himself. He didn't think he needed to fear God, because his theology reiterated that God would punish everyone else and not reprimand him. In his mind, he was anointed, he was purposed, and he was exempt from obedience. He lived in spiritual comfort where God was not a reality bigger than his own beliefs...and, as a result...Jonah, within his own mind, was untouchable.

And it's definitely not a secret to say this is a dangerous place to be.

How many of us behave with Jonah's same mentality? It is forever someone else's sin that is abominable, someone else's ways that are reprehensible to God, other people are told to repent, other people need to feel God, "hate the sin but love the sinner" ...but we think that, by some sort of divine providence, we can get away with anything. Christians need the reminder that we need to love other people and hate our own sins, examine ourselves first, and avoid getting so comfortable with the concepts that we have of God that we start protecting ourselves from His judgment. Jonah wasn't spared from the storm that hit. In that very moment, his theology failed him miserably.

It's easy to think we are favored of God and believe we do not have to obey His commands in our lives, even though they are there for our benefit (Psalm 19:8, Psalm 112:1, Zephaniah 2:3). This is an essential moment in the life of the believer, and especially, in the life of the leader, called to lead God's people. Every one of us was raised up in our faith, whether we started out as children or adults, to the point we are at now. We were taught to imply our own doctrines between the lines of Scripture, reading in what we were told we believed, whether it was true or Scriptural. We accepted what we were told, that we were unconditionally the "head and not the tail," that we can never lose our salvation, whether we want, esteem, or live it, or not, and that it's the "world" that's our problem. Jonah proves none of these things, cleverly implied between lines of Scripture, are principles that God has ever endorsed in the ways in which we teach them.

Christianity is not about being comfortable. We are not called to be a people who create God in the image of western civilization, upholding western values as superior to those of all other nations and looking down upon people of different income brackets, circumstances, or cultures. It's not about fashioning an idol that makes more people desire the things of the western world than the things of the Kingdom. Any time we start getting so comfortable that we ignore God's warnings, signs, and directives to us, we are going to have to face our the very real God of heaven and earth with a sign we don't like.

Jonah's experience also expounds on the role obedience plays in our witness with other people. How did it look that Jonah was blatantly fleeing from God, and such calamity came upon others? We're quick to want to wear the "Christian" label to stir up trouble or to fall back upon it in an argument to defend our position, but do we consider just how far that label extends when it's inconvenient for us? Everyone on the boat with Jonah knew he was fleeing God, and knew he was responsible for the storm that overtook the boat, caused those people to lose their cargo, and caused panic and fear. People are watching us, at all times, any time we decide to use the "Christian" label in our circumstances. Our obedience shows the way for them to be obedient. Our disobedience brings forth consequences for all, those watching as well as upon ourselves.

Jonah 1:11-17

The sea was getting rougher and rougher. So they asked him, "What should we do to you to make the sea calm down for us?" "Pick me up and throw me into the sea," he replied, "and it will become calm. I know that it is my fault that this great storm has come upon you." Instead, the men did their best to row back to land. But they could not, for the sea grew even wilder than before. Then they cried to the LORD, "O LORD, please do not let us die for taking this man's life. Do not hold us accountable for killing an innocent man, for You, O LORD, have done as You pleased." Then they took Jonah and threw him overboard, and the raging sea grew calm. At this the men greatly feared the LORD, and they offered a sacrifice to the LORD and made vows to Him. But the LORD provided a great fish to swallow Jonah, and Jonah was inside the fish three days and three nights.

(Related Bible references: Genesis 1:21, Genesis 9:6, Genesis 10:4, Psalm 65:2, Psalm 65:7, Psalm 89:9, Psalm 104:25, Psalm 107:29, Psalm 135:6)

I've been known to say that God either gives us a testimony or He makes an example of us. Jonah is a testimony of the truth to this statement. When Jonah decided to ignore the Lord, Jonah became an example of what happens when people (especially leaders, but by extension, all believers) ignore God. The others on the boat were more concerned for Jonah's well-being than Jonah was clearly concerned for them or for anyone else, for that matter. In Jonah's example, others saw God's intervention at hand and could see God's power and might at work.

When we don't have our relationship right with God, we enter a period of example, whereby we take our insights to the Throne and start to learn Who God really is, off paper rather than on. We experience God in trial so difficult and so intense, we realize we don't know God in the way we think we do. If Jonah truly knew God in the way he needed to in order to minister to the people of Nineveh, he would have simply trusted God and obeyed. The walls of doctrine, of confining theology set Jonah apart in a way that needed to shake up and shake out. He needed to be thrown overboard, sent to a time to think about what was needed and what was next. It wasn't enough for Jonah to admit this was his fault; more example needed to come. As soon as Jonah went to his place, his "time out," so to speak, the sea grew calm.

There we find Jonah, in the belly of the whale for three days and three nights, becoming an example, and experiencing God beyond the comfortable god of theism.

Chapter Two

Waiting for a Sign…
And Getting the One You Don't Want
(Jonah Chapter 2)

Key verses

- **Verse 2:** *He said: In my distress I called to the LORD, and He answered me. From the depths of the grave I called for help, and You listened to my cry.*

- **Verse 6:** *To the roots of the mountains I sank down; the earth beneath barred me in forever. But You brought my life up from the pit, O LORD my God.*

- **Verses 8-9:** *"Those who cling to worthless idols forfeit the grace that could be theirs. But I, with a song of thanksgiving, will sacrifice to You. What I have vowed I will make good. Salvation comes from the LORD."*

Words and phrases to know

- **Distress:** From the Hebrew word *tsarah,* which means, "straits, distress, trouble; vexer, rival wife."[2]

- **Depths of the grave:** From two Hebrew words: *beten*, which means, "belly, womb, body;"[2] and *she'owl,* which means, "sheol, underworld, grave, hell, pit."[3]

- **Deep:** From the Hebrew word *metsowlah*, which means, "depth, the deep, the deep sea."[4]

- **Seas:** From the Hebrew word *yam,* which means, "sea."[5]

- **Currents:** From the Hebrew word *nahar,* which means, "stream, river."[6]

- **Waves:** From the Hebrew word *mishbar,* which means, "breaker, breaking (of sea)."[7]

- **Breakers:** From the Hebrew word *gal,* which means, "heap, spring, wave, billow."[8]

- **Banished:** From the Hebrew word *garash,* which means, "to drive out, expel, cast out, drive away, divorce, put away, thrust away, trouble, cast up."[9]

- **Holy temple:** From two Hebrew words: *qodesh,* which means, "apartness, holiness, sacredness, separateness;"[10] and *heykal,* which means, "palace, temple, nave, sanctuary."[11]

- **Engulfing:** From the Hebrew word *'aphaph,* which means, "to surround, encompass."[12]

- **Pit:** From the Hebrew word *shachath,* which means, "pit, destruction, grave."[13]

- **Remembered:** From the Hebrew word *zakar*, which means, "to remember, recall, call to mind."[14]

- **Prayer:** From the Hebrew word *tephillah*, which means, "prayer."[15]

- **Worthless idols:** From two Hebrew words: *shav'*, which means, "emptiness, vanity, falsehood;"[16] and *hebel*, which means, "vapour, breath; vainly."[17]

- **Grace:** From the Hebrew word *checed*, which means, "goodness, kindness, faithfulness; a reproach, shame."[18]

- **Thanksgiving:** From the Hebrew word *towdah*, which means, "confession, praise, thanksgiving."[19]

- **Vowed:** From the Hebrew word *nadir*, which means, "to vow, make a vow."[20]

- **Salvation:** From the Hebrew word *yeshuw`ah*, which means, "salvation, deliverance."[21]

- **Vomited:** From the Hebrew word *qow'*, which means, "to vomit up, spue out, disgorge."[22]

Jonah 2:1-10

From inside the fish Jonah prayed to the LORD His God. He said: "In my distress I called to the LORD, and He answered me. From the depths of the grave I called for help, and You listened to my cry. You hurled me into the deep, into the very heart of the seas, and the currents swirled about me; all Your waves and breakers swept over me. I said, 'I have been banished from Your sight; yet I will look again toward Your holy temple.' The engulfing waters threatened me, the deep surrounded me; seaweed was wrapped around my head. To the roots of the mountains I sank down; the earth beneath barred me in forever. But You brought my life up from the pit, O LORD my God. When my life was ebbing away, I remembered You, LORD, and my prayer rose to You, to Your holy temple. Those who cling to worthless idols forfeit the grace that could be theirs. But I, with a song of thanksgiving, will sacrifice to You. What I have vowed I will make good. Salvation comes from the LORD." And the LORD commanded the fish, and it vomited Jonah onto dry land.

(Related Bible references: Exodus 3:14, 1 Samuel 12:21, 2 Chronicles 33:13, Job 33:24, Psalm 3:8, Psalm 5:7, Psalm 16:10, Psalm 17:6, Psalm 18:6, Psalm 22:24, Psalm 30:3, Psalm 33:9, Psalm 42:7, Psalm 50:14, Psalm 69:1, Psalm 91:15, Psalm 120:1, Psalm 130:1, Psalm 143:5, Ecclesiastes 5:4, Isaiah 12:2, Isaiah 26:16, Isaiah 38:17, Isaiah 50:2, Jeremiah 16:19, Lamentations 3:55, Hosea 5:15, Hosea 14:2, Habakkuk 2:18, Matthew 12:38-45, Matthew 16:1-4, Mark 8:11-13, Luke 11:29-32, Acts 2:27, Acts 2:31, Romans 12:1, 2 Corinthians 1:9, Hebrews 13:15)

In a literal sense, we could describe the book of Jonah as being about Jonah's discovery of the true and living God. Very little of the book of Jonah covers the prophecy he made to the people of Nineveh. Jonah didn't come to this understanding from studying theology or doctrine; he came to it by experience. God took him into the belly of the whale to allow him to die to himself and rise again new, truly born of God, with a change in his existential understanding.

As believers, we need to pay attention to the reality that Jonah came to know God in a powerful way after he was a "believer." He was a leader; he was someone who had clearly grown up in faith and had a certain level of intellect when it came to the things of God. He knew the voice of God in his life and knew the realities about God, but he didn't know God beyond his own limited intellectual understanding of Him. We don't talk about experience or the experience of God in Christianity much anymore. There are many reasons for this I would suspect, but I believe the most primary one is because we have replaced the experience of faith with intellectual understanding of God. I am not in any way putting down education in church or scholarship on spiritual matters, quite the opposite, in fact. I have spent many years advocating we return to educating clergy and believe we raise an unnecessary negative attitude against education. Education is not, in any way, the issue here; pride is.

Trying to turn God into a smart-sounding scientific argument is not faith, nor is it education. We are replacing the experience we can have with God, where we come to know God in a way that cannot be taken away from us, and replacing it with doctrines that make God suit our comforts and conveniences. If we take this vastly methodical or scientific approach to try and explain God, we can make God suit any one of our conveniences and understandings. This is not how God works. He doesn't fit into our convenient boxes of understanding. The result of such is never-ending bickering, defenses, and spiritual compromises, where God gets the burden to "prove" He is God to them.

More and more, we are hearing people "challenge" God today. This challenge is obvious among groups of atheists and agnostics. As public atheists and agnostics study the Bible and Christian history and pick apart the inconsistencies they discover as found in our doctrines and our claims, we hear outcry against their political demands and criticisms as the world seems to outwardly change. Christians look upon atheists and agnostics as godless heathens, individuals who are opposed to Christianity on all sorts of levels and simply want to abolish every single trace of God from our culture.

Christians need to stop fussing over secular battles and see the larger picture before us. The thing that needs to alarm Christians is the rate with which atheists and agnostics are winning over Christians with persuasive arguments and eloquent articulation. They are winning them over because all we are learning in church is to argue and articulate a god that defends our own lifestyles without truly coming to know God as He is. The result is the same approach to God that the atheist or agnostic may have: if You are God, then "prove" yourself.

- I'll believe (obey, follow, trust) in God if He heals me.

- I'll believe (obey, follow, trust) in God if He pays my bills.

- I'll believe (obey, follow, trust) in God if He sends me a sign.

- I'll believe (obey, follow, trust) in God if He gives me more money.

- I'll believe (obey, follow, trust) in God if He sends me a husband/wife/spouse.

- I'll believe (obey, follow, trust) in God if He gets me a better job.

- I'll believe (obey, follow, trust) in God if He gives me the family I always wanted.

- I'll believe (obey, follow, trust) in God if He performs a miracle.

- I'll believe (obey, follow, trust) in God if…if…if…

People who claim to be believers make statements like the ones above all the time. They will be "convinced" about God and following Him just as soon as God meets their demands. No better than an atheist or agnostic, their theology fails them when God doesn't meet their exclusive demands, by sending them their own "sign of Jonah" experience.

I've been asked many times as to why there doesn't seem to be an overabundance of miracles in our day and age. It does seem that, at different points in history, miracles were far more common than they are now. The reason why they are uncommon is because of this "prove Yourself, God!" mentality we now have. People expect God to go above and beyond to conform Himself to our whims, and He simply is not doing it. God is not to be played with, tested, or tried by humanity. God is neither insecure, nor uncertain of Who He is. In the face of such a trial, God will turn us over to experience, that we may experience Him and realize it's not the answer that we need, it's a change in our question. We need to humble ourselves before God to see His hand work in our lives, not expect Him to condescend Himself to our doctrines and theologies.

How much do we really believe in God today? Despite the sub-cultish nature of the church, afloat with Bible-themed movies, T-shirts, music, and television shows, do we believe in God when it hurts, when we don't get our own way, and when things seem to fall apart around us? Today's church is as defiant and challenging to God as Jonah was in his own ministry. When we "dare God to be God," we become disobedient. Even though we don't think of Jonah as challenging God, Jonah's actions were a huge challenge to God and His nature. By disobeying God, Jonah nothing short of dared God to show up and show out. He held forth to his conditions, showing no fear or concern that God might just not entertain what he was doing. Even when the other men on the boat grew fearful and concerned, Jonah held himself in a certain state of defiant being, not fearing there would be consequence. When the consequence came, he had to live with the results. Jonah didn't get an apology from God. He didn't recant His commands to Jonah, and He certainly didn't pacify Jonah's behavior. God never sat down and held Jonah's hand, telling him everything would be all right in the belly of the whale. He didn't make him feel better about himself. He took Jonah down to the depths, to a place where he would be thoroughly uncomfortable, awkward, and desolate, so that He could bring him back up again.

In Jonah's experience, he literally experienced what we call the "sign of Jonah." Before Jesus was crucified, He made mention of the "sign of Jonah":

Then some of the Pharisees and teachers of the law said to Him, "Teacher, we want to see a miraculous sign from You." He answered, "A wicked and adulterous generation asks for a miraculous sign! But none will be given it except the sign of the prophet Jonah. For as Jonah was three days and three nights in the belly of a huge fish, so the Son of Man will be three days and three nights in the heart of the earth. The men of Nineveh will stand up at the judgment with this generation and condemn it; for they repented at the preaching of Jonah, and now One greater than Jonah is here. The Queen of the South will rise at the judgment with this generation and condemn it; for she came from the ends of the earth to listen to Solomon's wisdom, and now one greater than Solomon is here. When an evil spirit comes out of a man, it goes through arid places seeking rest and does not find it. Then it says, 'I will return to the house I left.' When it arrives, it finds the house unoccupied, swept clean and put in order. Then it goes and takes with it seven other spirits more wicked than itself, and they go in and live there. And the final condition of that man is worse than the first. That is how it will be with this wicked generation." (Matthew 12:38-45)

The Pharisees and Sadducees came of Jesus and tested Him by asking Him to show them a sign from heaven. He replied, "When evening comes, you say, 'It will be fair weather, for the sky is red,' and in the morning, 'Today it will be stormy, for the sky is red and overcast.' You know how to interpret the appearance of the sky, but you cannot interpret the signs of the times. A wicked and adulterous generation looks for a miraculous sign, but none will be given it except the sign of Jonah." Jesus then left them and went away. (Matthew 16:1-4)

As the crowds increased, Jesus said, "This is a wicked generation. It asks for a miraculous sign, but none will be given it except the sign of Jonah. For as Jonah was a sign to the Ninevites, so also will the Son of Man be to this generation. The Queen of the South will rise at the judgment with the men of this generation and condemn them; for she came from the ends of the earth to listen to Solomon's wisdom, and now one greater than Solomon is here. The men of Nineveh will stand up at the judgment with this generation and condemn it; for they repented at the preaching of Jonah, and now One greater than Jonah is here." (Luke 11:30-32)

We know Jesus is speaking in His day of His own resurrection, lying in the grave for three days and three nights and then rising again to life forevermore. But this is not all Jesus was talking about, if we clearly understand the sign of Jonah from the literal experience of Jonah. The people of Jesus' day demanded a sign, much like people do today, and much like Jonah did when he disobeyed God. Jesus told them they would get no sign except the sign of Jonah: in other words, they would have an experience with God that would humble them to a point of realizing Who God is for themselves. They were about to get uncomfortable with God, face-to-face with their own shortcomings through the death and resurrection of Christ.

The sign of Jonah works the same way today. God brings us to a place where we get uncomfortable enough to confront ourselves. It's easy to believe in God when we make Him sound like large versions of ourselves, but in that moment when He asks us to do something and we choose not to do it, we suddenly learn that God is far bigger than we are. If we sincerely walk with God, we will all come to a place where our theologies will fail us. The creation of men to try and explain the nature of God, theology cannot replace the true nature of God, His true face and grace at work in our lives. We must decide to believe in God beyond us, beyond our understanding, beyond trying to figure it all out with human reasoning. It is coming to a place where we are not striving to accept God as an existence of men but accept God simply as He is. We learn that He is He Who has been, He Who is, and He Who will be (Exodus 3:14). He is beyond our time and space, the greatest of our wisdom and the greatest of our insights. When we come to accept this – He raises us up again – and we experience the sign of Jonah in our own life. It's not the sign we want or the miracle we seek, but God reveals Himself to us in a way that nobody can take away from us.

That was the result of Jonah's three days and three nights in the belly of the whale. Rather than looking down on him for that time he spent there, we need to realize there are those of us who have been in that place – in the belly of the whale – for far longer than three days and three nights. There are people who have been in such a place where God desires to make Himself real for years on end....and there they stay. Realizing God is greater than anything you have ever been taught or can conceive – and choosing to follow Him unto that end – is not a sign you are losing your faith. Jonah didn't lose his faith; he gained it, in a deeper and more powerful way. We can see Jonah's realization of God clearly and powerfully in Jonah chapter 2. He knew it was God that had the power to redeem, to lift up, to empower, and to bless. God was the same God of the storm as He was when Jonah came up from the waters, having been swallowed whole in the belly of the great fish. God was bigger than Jonah's convenience and his theological convictions. And, right within that moment when he found himself once again on dry land…Jonah experienced his own personal resurrection, overcoming the ways of man and ordered according to the necessary steps of faith to come.

Chapter Three

STUMBLING TO NINEVEH
(JONAH CHAPTER 3)

Key verses

- **Verses 1-2:** *The Word of the LORD came to Jonah a second time: "Go to the great city of Nineveh and proclaim to it the message I give you."*

- **Verse 5:** *The Ninevites believed God. They declared a fast, and all of them, from the greatest to the least, put on sackcloth.*

- **Verse 10:** *When God saw what they did and how they turned from their evil ways, he had compassion and did not bring upon them the destruction He had threatened.*

Words and phrases to know

- **Overturned:** From the Hebrew word *haphak*, which means, "to turn, overthrow, overturn."[1]

- **Sackcloth:** From the Hebrew word *saq,* which means, "mesh, sackcloth, sack."[2]

- **Dust:** From the Hebrew word *'epher,* which means, "ashes; worthlessness (fig.)."[3]

- **Decree:** From the Hebrew word *ta`am',* which means, "taste, judgment."[4]

- **Compassion:** From the Hebrew word *nacham,* which means, "to be sorry, console oneself, repent, regret, comfort, be comforted."[5]

- **Fierce anger:** From the Hebrew word *charown,* which means, "anger, heat, burning (of anger)."[6]

Jonah 3:1-2

Then the Word of the LORD came to Jonah a second time: "Go to the great city of Nineveh and proclaim to it the message I give you."

(Related Bible references: Jonah 1:1, John 1:1-2)

We know the message Jonah brought to Nineveh was one of repentance, unto the end of God's manifested mercy. That mercy was not just extended to Nineveh, however. Jonah experienced the mercy of God in the form of a second chance: a second chance to make it right, to do things over again and to follow God unto obedience.

The difference this time around with Jonah was to be obvious: Jonah knew God in a way he hadn't prior. He knew better than to try and outrun God. So, as much as Jonah still didn't like what he was asked to do, he still went ahead and did it.

Jonah stumbled himself to Nineveh. As we will see in chapter 4, he stumbled away from it, as well. Many of us, too, are stumbling on our way to where God would have us to be. Many of us also stumble away from our assignments in the end. Jonah reminds us we always have the opportunity to turn ourselves around and to do exactly what God would have us to do. In his very ministry, Jonah embodies the type of evangelist as well as the type of the evangelistic nature of the church. It is our purpose to present the Gospel and the life of the Kingdom to all God sends us to meet. Along that passage, we will stumble every time we don't know God for ourselves, in the way that we are able to experience Him. Even then, we may stumble at times. We won't always understand how God works, and what God tells us to do may not always make sense to us. God honors and blesses our obedience, even when we do it stumbling.

Jonah 3:3-5

Jonah obeyed the Word of the LORD and went to Nineveh. Now Nineveh was a very important city – a visit required three days. On the first day, Jonah started into the city. He proclaimed: "Forty more days and Nineveh will be overturned." The Ninevites believed God. They declared a fast, and all of them, from the greatest to the least, put on sackcloth.

(Related Bible references: Genesis 10:11, Ezra 8:21, Ezekiel 9:11, Joel 1:13, Zephaniah 2:13, Matthew 12:41, Luke 11:32)

Jonah cannot claim he felt like a failure in his ministry. The work he did saw results. We see where his prophetic work is clearly mentioned that when he gave a word, it brought about results. It wasn't the response others had to his work that was his problem. His ineffectiveness came in his avoidance to do exactly what God called him to do. It was a personal issue that caused hinderances in his obedience. When Jonah aligned with the will of God, knowing God in a deeper sense, Jonah went to Nineveh out of obedience. He proclaimed the word of repentance with such clarity, the people desired to align with God. His words pricked their hearts, convicted their minds, and caused them to believe God, now for themselves. Where Jonah dealt with unbelief and doubt, the people of Nineveh heard God's call…and they believed. The people of Nineveh prove how powerful belief is, and what belief should do in our lives.

We don't believe in God to change our economic status, gaining more things, a new car, a new house, or a bigger ministry; we believe in God to change our hearts, our minds, our states of being, the underlying essence of our lives and the issues we face as human beings. The first stage of belief is, undeniably, repentance. We are aware of where we find ourselves without God and we learn God is the answer to what we seek.

Repentance doesn't end because we become believers, as is clearly seen in Jonah's experience. He, too, had to repent of the ways in which he failed in his own life. He was just as much as sinner as every person in Nineveh, and he needed to realize that. Every time we stumble, we can go before God again to repent and turn ourselves toward Him, to see Him in our lives and encounter His grace and love within our own experience.

Jonah 3:6-10

When the news reached the King of Nineveh, he rose from his throne, took off his royal robes, covered himself with sackcloth and sat down in the dust. Then he issued a proclamation in Nineveh: "By the decree of the king and his nobles: Do not let any man or beast, herd or flock, taste anything; do not let them eat or drink. But let man and beast be covered with sackcloth. Let everyone call urgently on God. Let them give up their evil ways and their violence. Who knows? God may yet relent and with compassion turn from His fierce anger so that we will not perish." When God saw what they did and how they turned from their evil ways, He had compassion and did not bring upon them the destruction He had threatened.

(Related Bible references: Numbers 23:19, 2 Chronicles 16:9, Ezra 8:21, Psalm 2:10, Isaiah 1:16, Jeremiah 18:8, Ezekiel 18:21-23, Daniel 9:3, Joel 2:12-13, Malachi 3:6, Matthew 3:2, Matthew 3:8, Matthew 4:17, Matthew 11:21, Matthew 12:41, Luke 11:32, Acts 3:19, Acts 10:34, Romans 2:11)

In Jonah's ministry, we see clearly what it means to be "called to the nations." His ministry touched the people of Nineveh, from the greatest to the least. We tapped a little on this in terms of personality, but now we are going to look at what that call is and what that call means in terms of what being "called to the nations" looks like. Many people today use this term to describe their ministry today. They will speak of being "called to the nations" to describe their ministry as an international presence. Out of this number, many of these individuals believe that means their ministry will have a strong media presence, they will perform works before thousands of people, and that they will have the opportunity to travel to many people. There are some very key things that they cannot expound upon, however, using the term "called to the nations" in such a general way. Most do not know what that means, where they are called, where they are being sent to go, and do nothing to understand more about this call. The total distortion of this term means that those who are genuinely "called to the nations" do not understand exactly what it means and do not recognize how to prepare in order to bring this important work of ministry about.

- **Being "called to the nations…":** In Biblical times, being "called to the nations" meant an individual was called to minister and preach beyond the Hebrew people, the children of Israel. It was a reference of being "called to the Gentiles," which is another term for "nations." In our modern times, we can understand being "called to the nations" to mean being called beyond one's own immediate people or one's immediate comfort zone. Our faith is never an excuse to turn a blind eye to the rest of the world and to refrain from inviting them to come into a relationship with Christ and know the Gospel.

- **Knowing which "nations" one is assigned to go:** Being "called to the nations" is not a vague way of saying "I don't know what my assignment is," although that is how it is all-too-often used. When one was assigned to "nations," they knew exactly where they were supposed to go, whose lives they were supposed to impact, and the words that were to be delivered therein. If they weren't sure at first, they sought God and He revealed their course of direction.

- **Knowing about the nations they are assigned to:** Jonah knew the issues of the Assyrians. That was the precise reason why he didn't want to go to Nineveh. If someone is "called to the nations," it is essential they know the who, what, where, when, and why of those nations. Learning the language(s) of the nation or nations to which one is called, learning the economics, social structure, spiritual state, spiritual strongholds, social issues, customs, geography, and history are all essential to understand the people and convey that understanding as you proclaim God's message to them.

- **Humility:** You aren't going to go, no matter how much God tells you to go, if you haven't realized your position in light of God's authority and love in your life. Humility considers not only God's love for you, but God's love for others, as well, that needs to be poured out through you. Humility considers not only your status before God as our Creator, Redeemer, and Sustainer, but also what God wants to do through you for others.

- **Obedience:** Akin to humility is obedience. In humility, we do not esteem our own understanding higher than we ought. In the last chapter, we realized that God is beyond our own understanding, our own attempts to define Him, and our own thoughts and conceptions. That is because He is God, and we are not. If we love God and accept He is higher than we are and beyond our comprehension, we will do what He asks of us, even when we don't understand the "why."

- **Not biased:** The Scriptures tell us that God is not a "respecter of persons" (Acts 10:34, Romans 2:11). Those who are called to "nations" cannot go in obedience with prejudice of any form, racism, bigotry, or sexism. Such attitudes embrace the concept that God respects the individual's group or ideals above others, which is in direct context to the Gospel. If you are called to the nations, you are called to proclaim the message or do the ministry work, whether you may personally think such are worthy of the message or work, or not. God calls those with such issues to get over them.

Some argue that the book of Jonah argues that God "changes," saying this contradicts with verses that position He "changes not" (Malachi 3:6). God, indeed, does not change, but that also does not mean that He does not inspire a spirit of change or minister unto us the spirit of change. This is because at the very heart of God, we recognize and realize God is change. God is change in our lives; our positions in life; our realizations of who we are; and our ways of being that require us to find God in a deeper sense than mere theological musing. Repentance is a whole motivation of change, something God does within each of us, that is a part of our change. If God knows the end from the beginning, God knew the results of Jonah's preaching would bring about their repentance, and that they would ultimately come to seek God's face. This, likewise, does not make God a liar in the Word proclaimed (Numbers 23:19). The people of Nineveh still had the decision to make as to their repentance, and Jonah's prophecy was delivered in God's order to give them the opportunity to make their own decision based on the consequences that would result. He let Nineveh know that their current course of action would lead them astray, into a place of despair and destruction.

Evangelists are called to preach the heart of Christ, to make Him real in the lives of unbelievers and those who are away from the faith and show them that repentance is real. The evangelist, in his or her ministry, makes the promise of belief real to those who do not understand it. Jonah shows us how difficult the evangelistic work of the church is and how we must truly die to our own selves in flesh, concept, and ideal to reach out in the pursuit of others, that they may all know the Kingdom of heaven is at hand (Matthew 3:2, Matthew 4:17). In turn, the evangelist is also called to teach the church about this powerful and beautiful work among the Body of believers. There are ways to be effective – to reach the nations, as we discussed above – and ways to evangelize that are so ineffective, they will reach no one. In this hour, in this moment, support solid evangelists whose ministries are true and proven, and pray for God to raise up evangelists for the harvest in this day and age.

Chapter Four

THE GOD YOU DON'T HAVE TO UNDERSTAND...BECAUSE HE IS (JONAH CHAPTER 4)

Key verses

- **Verses 1-4:** *But Jonah was greatly displeased and became angry. He prayed to the LORD, "O LORD, is this not what I said when I was still at home? That is why I was so quick to flee to Tarshish. I knew that you are a gracious and compassionate God, slow to anger and abounding in love, a God Who relents from sending calamity. Now, O LORD, take away my life, for it is better for me to die than to live. But the LORD replied, "Have you any right to be angry?"*

- **Verses 8-9:** *When the sun rose, God provided a scorching east wind, and the sun blazed on Jonah's head so he grew faint. He wanted to die, and said, "It would be better for me to die than to live." But God said to Jonah, "Do you have a right to be angry about the vine?" "I do," he said. "I am angry enough to die."*

Words and phrases to know

- **Displeased:** From the Hebrew word *yara`*, which means, "to tremble, quiver."[1]

- **Angry:** From the Hebrew word *charah'*, which means, "to be hot, furious, burn, become angry, be kindled."[2]

- **Die:** From the Hebrew word *maveth,* which means, "death, dying, Death (personified), realm of the dead."[3]

- **Live:** From the Hebrew word *chay,* which means, "living, alive; relatives; life (abstract emphatic); living thing, animal; community."[4]

- **Right:** From the Hebrew word *yatab,* which means, "to be good, be pleasing, be well, be glad."[5]

- **Shelter:** From the Hebrew word *cukkah,* which means, "thicket, covert, booth."[6]

- **Vine:** From the Hebrew word *qiyqayown,* which means "a plant; perhaps a gourd, castor-oil plant, bottle-gourd."[7]

- **Discomfort:** From the Hebrew word *ra`,* which means "bad, evil; evil, distress, misery, injury, calamity; evil, misery, distress, injury."[8]

- **Worm:** From the Hebrew word *towla`,* which means "worm, scarlet stuff, crimson; worm, maggot."[9]

- **Scorching east wind:** From three Hebrew words: *chariyshiy,* which means "harsh, hot, sultry, silent (meaning uncertain);"[10] *qadiym,* which means, "east, east wind;"[11] and *ruwach,* which means "wind, breath, mind, spirit."[12]

- **Concerned:** From the Hebrew word *chuwc*, which means, "to pity, have compassion, spare, look upon with compassion."[13]

Jonah 4:1-4

But Jonah was greatly displeased and became angry. He prayed to the LORD, "O LORD, is this not what I said when I was still at home? That is why I was so quick to flee to Tarshish. I knew that You are a gracious and compassionate God, slow to anger and abounding in love, a God Who relents from sending calamity. Now, O LORD, take away my life, for it is better for me to die than to live." But the LORD replied, "Have you any right to be angry?"

(Related Bible references: Genesis 4:1-16, Genesis 35:18, Exodus 34:6, Numbers 11:15, 1 Kings 19:4, Job 6:9, Psalm 78:38, Psalm 86:5, Psalm 103:8, Psalm 145:8, Jeremiah 18:8, Ezekiel 33:11, Joel 2:13, Amos 7:3, Micah 7:18, Matthew 7:1-5, Matthew 20:1-15, Matthew 25:1-12, Luke 15:1-32, Romans 12:16, James 4:5)

We all know the story of the Prodigal Son in Luke 15:11-32:

Jesus went on to say, "There was once a man who had two sons. The younger one said to him, 'Father, give me my share of the property now.' So the man divided his property between his two sons. After a few days the younger son sold his part of the property and left home with the money. He went to a country far away, where he wasted his money in reckless living. He spent everything he had. Then a severe famine spread over that country, and he was left without a thing. So he went to work for one of the citizens of that country, who sent him out to his farm to take care of the pigs. He wished he could fill himself with the bean pods the pigs ate, but no one gave him anything to eat. At last he came to his senses and said, 'All my father's hired workers have more than they can eat, and here I am about to starve! I will get up and go to my father and say, "Father, I have sinned against God and against you. I am no longer fit to be called your son; treat me as one of your hired workers."' So he got up and started back to his father. "He was still a long way from home when his father saw him; his heart was filled with pity, and he ran, threw his arms around his son, and kissed him. 'Father,' the son said, 'I have sinned against God and against you. I am no longer fit to be called your son.' But the father called to his servants. 'Hurry!' he said. 'Bring the best robe and put it on him. Put a ring on his finger and shoes on his feet. Then go and get the prize calf and kill it, and let us celebrate with a feast! For this son of mine was dead, but now he is alive; he was lost, but now he has been found.' And so the feasting began. "In the meantime the older son was out in the field. On his way back, when he came close to the house, he heard the music and dancing. So he called one of the servants and asked him, 'What's going on?' 'Your brother has come back home,' the servant answered, 'and your father has killed the prize calf, because he got him back safe and sound.' The older brother was so angry that he would not go into the house; so his father came out and begged him to come in. But he spoke back to his father, 'Look, all these years I have worked for you like a slave, and I have never disobeyed your orders. What have you given me? Not even a goat for me to have a feast with my friends! But this son of yours wasted all your property on prostitutes, and when he comes back home, you kill the prize calf for him!' 'My son,' the father answered, 'you are always here with me, and everything I have is yours. But we had to celebrate and be happy, because your brother was dead, but now he is alive; he was lost, but now he has been found.'" (GNT)

The beautiful paintings, messages of promise about those who were lost, and now found, and hope for those who are wayward or away from the faith tug at our heartstrings every time this passage comes into focus. The one we have never heard a message about was the son who was not the prodigal, who remained with the father while the prodigal son went on his merry way. The story tells us he was indignant of his brother's return, angry because a fuss was made over his brother when he was the "good son," the one who had done right for many years and felt he never received the reward.

And, as we study this text year after year and skirt over the other brother, I wonder if he was wrong.

We don't hear about the brother of the prodigal because he hits too close to home. Many people in Christianity grow angry when a new member is celebrated or grow despondent when they do not feel they receive their just do, having devoted how many years or how much time to the Lord and the church. Their focus is on their works rather than on their faith. So much of their lives is spent being "the good one," they forget to believe beyond a strict doctrine that exempts them from self-examination. They grow indignant.

The brother of the prodigal son is not the only one in the Bible who we could describe as "indignant." The workers who showed up early to work in the vineyard (Matthew 20:1-15), the foolish virgins waiting for the bridegroom (Matthew 25:1-12), Cain when Abel's sacrifice was accepted and his was not (Genesis 4:1-16), and yes, even the one we are devoting this study to, Jonah, are all examples of people who took issue with the way God handled matters. They felt God should do things one way, not rightly understanding the heart and nature of God, or seeing the many ways in which God has been merciful to them throughout the years.

Jonah gives himself – and his indignant motives – away here, in verses 1-4. He would rather have died than see the people of Nineveh come to know God, in repentance. He was willing to risk his own relationship with God and the lives of others to make sure that God's mercy and love didn't extend to Nineveh. This has an all-too-familiar ring when we consider where the church is, today. I've met people who literally believe some people do not deserve to hear the Gospel or to have the opportunity to repent, because of what they feel they've done. In the place of being indignant, individuals take on a nature of judgment that it is best to beware. Being a Christian means that we step aside and allow God His full decision and power when it comes to judgment (Matthew 7:1-5). We recognize we have been forgiven our sins, and that what God can do for us in our lives, He can do for others.

God doesn't, once again, let Jonah off the hook for his attitude. He outright asks Jonah, "Do you have any right to be angry?" That is God's response to indignant attitudes among believers. It is what He has to say to each and every one of us who gets ourselves in a snit because God extends His mercy, love, and forgiveness to someone we don't think deserves it. Running off every which way, protesting the love of God by feeling life is not worth living if God extends mercies to someone else, is not going to change God, nor move Him to our persuasions. Save the time, the effort, and the protests…and trust God, even when you don't understand Him.

Jonah 4:5-10

Jonah went out and sat down at a place east of the city. There he made himself a shelter, sat in its shade and waited to see what would happen to the city. Then the LORD God provided a vine and made it grow over Jonah to give shade for his head to ease his discomfort, and Jonah was very happy about the vine. But at dawn the next day God provided a worm, which chewed the vine so that it withered. When the sun rose, God provided a scorching east wind, and the sun blazed on Jonah's head so that he grew faint. He wanted to die, and said, "It would be better for me to die than to live." But God said to Jonah, "Do you have a right to be angry about the vine?" "I do," he said. "I am angry enough to die." But the LORD said, "You have been concerned about this vine, though you did not tend it or make it grow. It sprang up overnight and died overnight. But Nineveh has more than a hundred and twenty thousand people who cannot tell their right hand from their left, and many cattle as well. Should I not be concerned about that great city?"

(Related Bible references: Deuteronomy 28:39, 1 Kings 19:4, Psalm 36:6, Psalm 103:10, Psalm 103:13, Psalm 121:5, Psalm 145:9, Isaiah 40:7, Ezekiel 17:10, Ezekiel 19:12, Hosea 13:15, Amos 8:13, Matthew 18:33, John 3:30)

If nothing else, Jonah was persistent and consistent. He set himself up in a cushy spot to watch the judgment fall on Nineveh, a judgment that never came in the way he desired. He was determined to watch the downfall of his perceived enemies, rooted in political and social embitterment. He didn't care about individuals, about people, about the souls of men that were at stake and was not even glad that his ministry attempts were successful.

Arguing with God is about as effective as trying to spar with your shadow. We can argue with God, and just stay put, and stay where we are, until we relent our will to His. In Chapter 4, God illustrated to Jonah how He is God. He is the One Who planted the vine, sent the worm, sent the wind, the sun, and the shade. As the Creator, it was His decision, and no one else's, to be merciful as He desired to be merciful. It was God Who knew the situation of the people of Nineveh, their own confusions, their own spiritual blindness as idolaters, and their own economic state as human beings. Behind every bigotry, every sullen or angry state, and yes, every judgment of ours, there are people who have the same needs, longings, and need for direction in their lives, just as we do. God is the answer for them, just as He is for us.

How do we express our faith and its manifestation in our lives, even when we don't like what God tells us to do? Jonah argued with God, and remained indignant, even after his obedience. Jonah still didn't "get it." He'd come face-to-face with God, did what God asked of him, and he was still in a place where he threw a tantrum. Jonah still sat there, wanting to die, and pouting (as seems to be his pattern) when God confronted him with questions he did not want to answer.

God is asking these same questions to us, today, about people, places, nations, and things…and we still do not want to answer. The longer we wait, the longer we play with God, the more He will put us in a position to examine…and answer…for ourselves. Just as abruptly as the book of Jonah seems to end, the questions for us, begin. We may never understand the fullness of God's nature or His long-suffering toward us, but at the same time, Jonah teaches us that we don't have to understand God. Part of knowing, believing in, and understanding God beyond our own theological propositions is recognizing we will never understand God in totality, because He is beyond our own level of comprehension. Embracing God as God, as the One Who was, and Who is, and Who is to come, outside of time, space, and human reasoning can transform everything in our own lives: our walk with Him, our interactions with others, and the way in which we see the Kingdom of God. It is time for us to rise up from the belly of the whale, unto new life, and unto one that is more humble, accepting that when we take part in the life of God, we adapt this eternal nature unto ourselves, and, too, become a part of something beyond our own understanding as He increases within us, and we decrease in our own need for self (John 3:30). No matter how many times we stumble on the way to where we are going, God is always there to restore us, as we trust and believe in Him.

References

Opening Quotations

[1]Tillich, Paul. *Systematic Theology, Vol. 1: Reason And Revelation, Being And God*. Chicago, Illinois: The University of Chicago Press, 1951.

[2]Hillsong United,, *"Oceans (Where Feet May Fail)."* Matt Crocker, Lance Adkins, Joel Houston and Salmon Ligthelm.

Introduction

"Book Of Jonah." http://en.wikipedia.org/wiki/Book_of_Jonah. Accessed October 9, 2014.

Chapter One

[1] <u>Strong's Exhaustive Concordance of the Bible</u>, #1697
[2] Ibid., #3068
[3] Ibid., #3124
[4] Ibid, #5210
[5] Ibid., #7121
[6] Ibid., #5927
[7] Ibid., #7451
[8] Ibid., #1272
[9] Ibid., #8659
[10] Ibid., #3305
[11] Ibid., #1419
[12] Ibid., #5591

[13] Ibid., #3372
[14] Ibid., #7290
[15] Ibid., #5307
[16] Ibid., #1486
[17] Ibid., #5680
[18] Ibid., #7945
[19] Ibid., #2077
[20] Ibid., #1709
[21] Ibid., #1104
[22] Ibid., #7969
[23] Ibid., #3117
[24] Ibid., #7969
[25] Ibid., #3915
[26] Ibid., #3124

Chapter Two

[1] Strong's Exhaustive Concordance of the Bible, #6869
[2] Ibid, #0990
[3] Ibid., #7585
[4] Ibid., #4688
[5] Ibid., #3220
[6] Ibid., #5104
[7] Ibid., #4867
[8] Ibid., #1530
[9] Ibid., #1644
[10] Ibid., #6944
[11] Ibid., #1964
[12] Ibid., #0661
[13] Ibid., #7845
[14] Ibid., #2142
[15] Ibid., #8605
[16] Ibid., #7723
[17] Ibid., #1892
[18] Ibid., #2617
[19] Ibid., #8426
[20] Ibid., #5087
[21] Ibid., #3444
[22] Ibid., #6958

Chapter Three

[1] Strong's Exhaustive Concordance of the Bible, #2015
[2] Ibid., #8242
[3] Ibid, #0665
[4] Ibid., #2940
[5] Ibid., #5162
[6] Ibid., #2740

Chapter Four

[1] <u>Strong's Exhaustive Concordance of the Bible</u>, #3415
[2] Ibid., #2734
[3] Ibid, #4194
[4] Ibid., #2416
[5] Ibid., #3190
[6] Ibid., #5521
[7] Ibid., #7021
[8] Ibid., #7451
[9] Ibid., #8438
[10] Ibid., #2759
[11] Ibid., #6921
[12] Ibid., #7307
[13] Ibid., #2347

About the Author

DR. LEE ANN B. MARINO, PH.D., D.MIN., D.D.

Dr. Lee Ann B. Marino, Ph.D., D.Min., D.D. (she/her) is "everyone's favorite theologian" leading Gen X, Millennials, and Gen Z with expertise in leadership training, queer and feminist theology, general religion, and apostolic theology. She has served in ministry since 1998 and was ordained as a pastor in 2002 and an apostle in 2010. She founded what is now Sanctuary Apostolic Fellowship Empowerment (SAFE) Ministries in 2004. Under her ministry heading Dr.
Marino is founder and Overseer of Sanctuary International Fellowship Tabernacle (SIFT) (the original home of National Coming Out Sunday) and The Sanctuary Network, and Chancellor of Apostolic Covenant Theological Seminary (ACTS).

Affectionately nicknamed "the Spitfire," Dr. Marino has spent over two decades as an "apostle, preacher, and teacher" (2 Timothy 1:11), exercising her personal mandate to become "all things to all people" (1 Corinthians 9:22). Her embrace of spiritual issues (both technical and intimate) has found its home among both seekers and believers, those who desire spiritual answers to today's issues.

Dr. Marino has preached throughout the United States, Puerto Rico, and Europe in hundreds of religious services and experiences throughout the years. A history maker in her own right, she has spent over two decades in advocacy, education, and work for and within minority spiritual communities (including African American, Hispanic, and LGBTQ+). She has also served as the first woman on all-male synods, councils, and panels, as well as the first preacher or speaker welcomed of a different race, sexual orientation, or identity among diverse communities. Today, Dr. Marino's work extends to over 150 countries as she hosts the popular *Kingdom Now* podcast, which is in the top 20 percentile of all podcasts worldwide. She is also the author of over 35 books and the popular Patheos column, *Leadership on Fire*. To date, she has had five bestselling titles within their subject matter: *Understanding Demonology, Spiritual Warfare, Healing, and Deliverance: A Manual for the Christian Minister*; *Ministry School Boot Camp: Training for Helps Ministries, Appointments, and Beyond*; *Discovering Intimacy: A Journey Through the Song of Solomon*; *Fruit of the Vine: Study and Commentary on the Fruit of the Spirit*; and *Ministering to LGBTQ+ (and Those Who Love Them): A Primer for Queer Theology* (and its accompanying workbook).

As a public icon and social media influencer, Dr. Marino advocates healthy body image (curvy/full-figured), representation as a demisexual/aromantic, and albinism awareness as a model. Known to those she works with, she is a spiritual mom, teacher, leader, professor, confidant, and friend. She continues to transform, receiving new teaching, revelation, and insight in this thing we call "ministry." Through years of spiritual growth and maturity, Dr. Marino stands as herself, here to present what God has given to her for any who have an ear to hear.

For more information, visit her website at kingdompowernow.org.

www.ingramcontent.com/pod-product-compliance
Lightning Source LLC
Chambersburg PA
CBHW071415040426
42444CB00009B/2266